Swift Happenings

A Poetry Collection
by
Chloe Hanks

Lovely Betty,

thank you for your
words and for taking
time over mine.
With love,
Chloe xo

Swift Happenings

Chloe Hanks

Edited by Chloe Hanks

First published in 2023 by Chloe Hanks
clhankspoetry.bigcartel.com

Instagram: C.L.Hanks
Twitter: ChloeHanks4
TikTok: PhDDiaries23

Cover Photograph and Design
by Lydia Joy Dronsfield & Chloe Hanks

Instagram: lydia.joy.designs

"If music be the food of love, play on"—
William Shakespeare, Twelfth Night

Introduction

In December 2019, music legend and critically acclaimed songwriter, Taylor Swift, published a poem. British Vogue shared, 'The Trick to Holding On', an exclusive publication from Swift which contained a step-by-step guide to 'reinvention'. Only months prior, Swift had self-published a heart-wrenching testimony to her social media explaining her loss of the ownership of her first six studio albums. Shortly after this event, she began to re-record those albums. Her re-records *Fearless (Taylor's Version)* and *Red (Taylor's Version)* have outsold the original editions of the albums and quickly grasped the attention of the world, prompting artists and writers alike to consider why legal ownership is so important to creatives.

As a lifelong fan, I was devastated by the loss of Swift's ownership; feeling myself as though something had been stolen, be it the music or my memories. As a writer, however, I was engrossed in this complex legal battle. How could it be that somebody could simply purchase the ownership of someone else's words? Arguably, Swift's passion for this case is rooted not only in a decade and a half of hard work, but also in the fact that her songs come from an intimate place of vulnerability and lived experience. With this being said, I found something incredibly poignant in that her song writing credit appeared to be her saving grace in allowing her to recreate her albums.

Swift Happenings is a collection in response to this controversy, but the poems have emerged from my lived experience and the memories I have gathered growing up with Taylor's music. Each poem exists in response to an isolated Taylor Swift lyric. My words exist in conversation with hers. The stain of ink pressed into the crevasses of our palms cannot be bought from our fingertips by strangers in corporate suits.

As a fan, I wanted to echo her efforts and reclaim the memories I have associated to each lyric after well over a decade of following her career. As a writer, I wanted to explore the poetry in those lyrics and aim to emphasise the power of legacy. Swift's ownership may have been legally forced into question; however, her authorship will always be protected by the legacy she has built, and the love people have for her music. This was illustrated in the Rolling Stone Magazine review of *Red (Taylor's Version)* whereby the publication stated she "[made] a classic even better."[1]

At the time of the publication of *Swift Happenings*, Taylor Swift has re-recorded two of her six albums for which she lost ownership, as above: *Fearless (Taylor's Version)* and *Red (Taylor's Version)*. Consequently, poems inspired by *Taylor Swift, Speak Now, 1989* and *Reputation* are referenced to the original albums. Should you find this collection sometime in the future, and Taylor has completed her endeavour to reclaim her words, please stream/purchase/acknowledge Taylor's Versions.

with love,

Chloe

---

[1] *'Red (Taylor's Version)' Makes a Classic Even Better – Rolling Stone (Rob Sheffield, 2021, Rollingstone.com)*

Dedication

This collection is for my mum, for purchasing me my first Taylor Swift album, *Fearless*, in 2009 after I finally let the dentist look at my teeth. I have often wondered if this is a decision she went on to regret, given that I have listened to little else aside from Taylor Swift's discography since.

For my dad, for his efforts to offer any other music to my library, however futile this may have been. Also, for teaching me to play guitar so that I could write songs for a while. I am not sure I would be writing poems now if the music hadn't come first.

For my younger sister, for being forced to hear Taylor Swift over and over again: I am sure she is a Swiftie in denial now because of it.

Lastly, this is a collection for anyone who cannot listen to a Taylor Swift song without subsequently thinking about me. It is a unique power that Taylor Swift fans have, and it never fails to make me smile.

Contents

tell them my name[2]

They doubted the weight of her quill and ink,
too shallow the scratches on paper; in response
she wrote an entire record of lyrics
completely by herself.

> She was nineteen.

In response, they delved into the anonymity
behind her subject matter, attaching labels to faceless figures
and undermining the craft.

> A decade passed,

In the shadow of a gloomy office,
fingers hovered over a typewriter,
a faceless figure got to decide on the fate of the words
and where they should reside—

> but ink stains.

You cannot erase the way it presses into your palm and gives
you away— composition is not a cause for debate.

They cannot stop us from hearing the words
> and speaking her name.

---

[2] *Inspired by the lyric 'when they point to the pictures, please tell them my name' written by Taylor Swift for her song 'Long Live' featured on the album Speak Now.*

youth[3]

Have you ever had a memory
present itself like a visual trail?

You turn your head in a certain light
and see the fragments of a day long passed.

A kaleidoscope, not induced by an acid trip
but rather the significant weight of a lyric;

suddenly you are once again fourteen
and desperate to know what it feels like to be loved.

A while ago I was eight years old
and she was seventeen—

my mum bought the album for me
because I had behaved well at the dentist.

I'd bared my teeth, crossed my arms
and closed my eyes until it was over.

My reward was her. Now every moment
I have it in me to remember is framed by the words

that she shaped, the one thread of consistency
amongst fickle friends, migrating like birds in winter,

faceless lovers that went cold wrapped up
in long discarded bed sheets. I have known nothing

and nobody that could hold me quite like this,

---

[3] *Inspired by the lyric 'we were both young' written by Taylor Swift for her song Love Story featured on the album Fearless (Swift's Version).*

in the palm of a hand I have never held.

Yet I have memorised every sound;
the melody to her figuring things out.

***remember it*[4]**

                              my lyric booklet
             folded down the middle
                    to isolate which part of each song
I was attempting to memorise
                         that day

it was, in some way,
                              my first taste of poetry

                    she was fearless
        I was powerful
                    the pages are calloused
                              with days and weeks
     of dampening:
                    the oils from my fingertips

        created a memory—
                    in my long-lost bedroom,
hear me sing
                              the poetry.

[4] *Inspired by the lyric 'capture it, remember it' written by Taylor Swift for her song 'Fearless' featured on the album Fearless (Swift's Version).*

flashback[5]

A flick of the wrist
and the water rains down,
me: crossed legged beneath
and somewhat buried.

I echo the melody
of a love story into the
endless shower stream.
I claim my moments
peace.

My family have each lyric
etched into their memory.
A few years would pass
before I took my place
centre stage to tell the tale
again.

With the glow of a fairy
tale in my dizzy brown eyes,
I made my mother cry.

---

[5] *Inspired by the lyric 'I close my eyes and the flashback starts' written by Taylor Swift for her song Love Story featured on the album Fearless (Swift's Version).*

faded picture[6]

Summers were auburn: arriving for a taste
in early May and then shying away again
until burning July. My skin kissed by an olive
would glow to a golden brown and life seemed
better somehow.

My world existed entirely in daydreams,
make believe inside a closed off mind. All
the time in the world was mine. I stained
my favourite jeans with freshly cut grass
and my best friend inked them with a smiley
face.

I had a crush on a boy who talked to me
at school once and everything was so alive—
as though the heat emblazoned each feeling
into a fire. My best friend and I laid ourselves
flat beneath the picture-filled clouds
and wondered how long this infatuation
might take to erupt into happily-ever-after love.

I saw no inkling in the storybook sky that
in only a few months' time she would deem
my company insufficient; or, that it would
take me until the following summer to see
this love and become indifferent.

Summer was echoed with the year that
all of my daydreams faded like the clouds
that fell from the sky; and I started
to question what I wanted from life.

---

[6] Inspired by the lyric 'the faded picture of a beautiful night' written by Taylor Swift for
her song 'The Other Side of the Door' featured on her album Fearless (Swift's Version).

white horse[7]

there was so much love
cross-stitched like memories
in the shape of her lyrics
that for a good decade
I truly believed in love

the kind you find in
fairy tales and Netflix
specials. it was fed to
me gently before I
could even comprehend

the double-edged sword
she was bearing. there
were messages in the
track list and I was
not listening—

> *nothing cuts quite*
> *as deep as the reins*
> *across your palms*
> *as you wait, horse backed,*
> *and patient—for a prince.*

---

[7] *Inspired by the lyric 'it's too late for you and your white horse to come around' written by Taylor Swift for her song 'White Horse' featuring on the album Fearless (Swift's Version).*

lights go down[8]

Thirteen years old ached like a broken limb
and I spent so many nights cocooned in blankets
watching her sing.
                         I had headphones in.
There was no one to share the screen with,   just
me, and Taylor Swift.   The stage would open,
and thrust her into the air like   a butterfly caught
on wind. Her white sleeves billowing   like wings.
                       Fifty thousand
people   or more erupted into chaos and the pain
was lost. I could not fathom that many   minds
alert to those whimsical words of mine, that many
hearts alive to care.
                 No one even wanted to sit
with me at lunchtime. From that moment onward,
I wanted to write.
           To create a legacy that could only
be mine, to draw them in to everything that made
me weak,
          because Taylor told me to *speak*.

---

[8] *Inspired by the lyric 'hit me with those green eyes, baby, as the lights go down' written by Taylor Swift for her song 'Sparks fly' on her album Speak Now.*

I used to write songs, part I[9]

Guitar strings cut
into your fingerprints
when you first start writing songs,
like they have to take something from you
in order to understand
how to proceed.

I used to write songs
because Taylor wrote songs.
I was fourteen and I wanted to be like her
because she was magic. I liked the bounce of her curls
as she spun around on stage
with the rhinestones on her guitar
twinkling beneath the lights.

I used to write songs
because when I was writing songs,
I wasn't thinking about how I used to daydream.
When you are writing songs,
everything else becomes
secondary.

I used to write songs
because my friends didn't write songs.
I liked living a life that no one else was living;
it was like something special might happen
if I just kept on singing.

---

[9] *Inspired by the lyric 'all those other girls, well they're beautiful, but would they write a song for you?' written by Taylor Swift for her song 'Hey Stephen' for her album* Fearless *(Swift's Version).*

9

growing up[10]

It was always about love. Always.
In a childlike way; fairy-tales and American pre-teen films.
I truly believed it would be like that for both of us.

She and I. Her and me.
Each time she almost found it and I trailed behind her
with whatever hopeless teenager could fill the shadow

of Taylor's lover.

I thought it so unfair when they said she collected
too many boys when all of the girls around me could
count just as many. Isn't this how it works?

You collect and gather and explore
until you find the one that is yours.

The pair of us grew up slowly and she realised
quicker than I; the failures set up in the fairy tales
and the cruelty in plotlines as they come undone.

The futility in searching endlessly
for the chosen one.

---

[10] Inspired by the lyric 'growing up and falling in love' written by Taylor Swift for her song 'Mary's Song' featured on her debut album Taylor Swift.

I / coax you into paradise[11]

He and I were reckless.
Me, with my skeletal limbs secluded
in my school blazer sleeves and he,
collecting me—

no one else's boyfriend drove a car.

I trod my careful footsteps over
his hardwood floors, shushed myself
into silence, so in love I thought
I was dying.

He silenced me to a secret with the image
of everything I had ever wanted:

I took the oath upon the tip of my tongue.
Until soon enough, the winds changed,
and he disappeared with a migration
of birds alighting like clouds.

Still barefoot, and silent
I looked around at the magic only
I could see and wondered
how I might ever let another man in
when the root of this whole happenstance
was him.

---

[11] *Inspired by the lyric 'do you miss the rogue who coaxed you into paradise and left you there?' written by Taylor Swift for her song 'Coney Island' featuring on her album Evermore.*

11

I / screaming colour[12]

At some stage in the stillness after 1989,
I realised I could switch off my feelings.

Things were stagnant anyway
my heart long broken and aching in that dull kind of way,

I settled myself on the living room sofa and stayed there
all summer, daydreaming about starting over.

I just did not know how, and you would visit me in ways
that were almost cruel as though you knew I felt nothing

aside from the absence of the pair of you—

you picked me up and we watched her sing together
and she told the entire crowd the extent to which I deserved
better,

it took a few years for the memories to fade
and now there's nothing I do better than running away.

---

[12] Inspired by the lyric 'the rest of the world was black and white but we were in
screaming colour' written by Taylor Swift for her song 'Out of the Woods' featured on
her album 1989.

a tough crowd[13]

I must hate women because I love Taylor Swift.
She is flawed in the same way I am, yet somehow,
she is flawed in a way the world will not allow.
Girls at school would insult me by insulting Taylor Swift.
I must be fake because I love Taylor Swift.
Should she ever be mentioned,
they would turn to me and stare
because all I had to offer was my love of Taylor Swift.
She and I were one—
and both unworthy in some sense of the word.

These days, they talk of the planet
as though they are perfectly trying to defend it
and I must want it to die because I love Taylor Swift.
They talk of politics, old friends hate me
because feminism is still imperfect, and I love Taylor Swift.

They think I love whiteness because I love Taylor Swift.

They think I'm a girl boss because I love Taylor Swift.

They think I am basic because I love Taylor Swift.

Taylor Swift is a person and I love Taylor Swift.

---

[13] Inspired by the lyric 'life is a tough crowd' written by Taylor Swift for her song 'Innocent' featured on the album Speak Now.

II / the girl in the dress[14]

The midnight that I turned nineteen, my boyfriend helped himself to me. I found myself pressed so callously against the wall of the club as the music reverberated and I went numb. He called it love. I can still hear the words he called out above the music, *it's fine—*

she's my girlfriend. Shortly after 1am, I was walking myself home in a city I did not yet know and when I made it safely to my bed, I let her sing me, gently, to sleep.

Days later, he mentioned that I didn't finish as often as I used to. When I think about it now, I like to imagine I told him how I no longer cared to pretend to.

---

[14] *Inspired by the lyric 'the girl in the dress cried the whole way home' written by Taylor Swift for her song 'Dear John' featuring on the album Speak Now.*

14

party dress[15]

We were all three dangled in a chain
of birthdays like bunting along a dull, grey wall.
Celebrations came one day for us all: my house
littered with my sisters' closest friends.
Yet none of mine came. I cradled myself
into the bottom of my wardrobe because
I did not yet know how to cope with
not being worthy of celebration.

A few years came and sped by
and I always ended up thrust into
my white, school shirt instead of a birthday
dress. That year I was stood up
by my very best friend who wanted
to have lunch with her boyfriend.

At sixteen my parents surprised me with
the man I'd been dating. In my minds' eye
he grins at me from across the cutlery
because we both know what
this birthday means.

Nineteen and I crumbled between the
fingertips of a man who spent my birthday
kneading me with words like *bitch*;
he couldn't afford a gift, a card—
just his forceful kiss
and the following week
he bought all his friends paintball tickets.

---

[15] *Inspired by the lyric 'standing there in my party dress' written by Taylor Swift for her song 'the Moment I Knew' featured on the album Red (Swift's Version).*

Slowly things whittle down until
you are always
some sort of alone.
When I turned twenty-three
my mother said to me
*birthdays do get quite sad
when you are grown.*

clandestine meetings[16]

We move through life
as scavengers, collecting moments
and oftentimes people.
Lovers become flowers
pressed between scrap book pages.

I try to categorise mine,
both in colour and petal
but, also, the pattern of *her life*.
As I root through the lyric booklets

I underline the similarities
between her tales and mine.
I gather the little parallels—
two parallels
and you have identified a direction.

I glamorised my first kiss
into something fearless,
neglecting to consider the missed match.
The red flags.
I should have felt alarm

where instead,
I succumbed to the magic
she said I would feel.
It's not her fault.
I chose the touch;
sought him out

with my rose-tinted lips,
my delicate limbs

[16] Inspired by the lyric 'clandestine meetings and longing stares' written by Taylor Swift for her song 'Illicit Affairs' featuring on her album Folklore.

hidden beneath my school blazer.
I classify each man
I have known into
a beaten-up CD.

Why is it
the more we yearn
for a pastel rainbow lover,
the more we find ourselves
engrossed by dull, grey men
readying themselves
like leeches.

I toss and I turn
in someone else's bed sheets
and hope that, one day,
I might feel at home in them.

Everything falls into place
if you treat life with patience:
you only need two parallels
to create a direction.

hear my stolen lullabies[17]

In the making of 1989,
she sampled her own heartbeat
into the rhythm of
a song.

A beat that echoes
beyond the constraints
of a melody—

years later,
I woke to find my ears ringing.
There were lyrics melting
from my fingertips, dripping
to the floor as I rose from my bed.

Words spilled as I walked
to meet the bathroom mirror,
I skipped around
each   blank space.

Soon I was frozen,
time went on in a moment
of uncertainty as I saw her lyrics
spilling from me. Her heartbeat
ringing in my ears.

Puddles of ink
were accumulating
beneath my feet, spreading
and spilling
down the stairs to the door;

---

[17] *Inspired by the lyric 'when you can't sleep at night, you'll hear my stolen lullabies' written by Taylor Swift for her song 'My Tears Ricochet' featuring on her album Folklore.*

19

as if summoned
by an external force.

Cities away,
goblins were sheltering in dingy,
New York back streets,
drawing the words in.

The only way
we could salvage
that beat was to sing
back the words that had pooled
at our feet.

III | *I used to write songs, part 2*[18]

I used to write songs
before I met my boyfriend.
He likes the silk of my voice when I sing
but he doesn't like the tales
of the boys who came
before him.

I used to write songs
because it made the pain
seem warranted: strangers would
tell me I was talented.

I used to write songs
because the man I loved
back then was writing them too,
but now I am the only one
living in a melody
and it gets lonely.

The music
was pulled from me
as though I gave away my soul
to the strings on the guitar
I played for him.

I haven't written
a song in years.

The words came back, in time—
but the music never did.

---

[18] *Inspired by the lyric 'with every guitar string scar on my hand' written by Taylor Swift for her song 'Lover' featuring on the album Lover.*

III | *a lovely bride*[19]

        white silk dresses
lace & sparkle
                like a princess
        I could have married him
it would have been *fine*, babies to share
at Christmas time
              I did not feel
like a princess, I didn't feel fine, I felt
      like a child
           in her mum's
white dress
I felt a blank space where I should have
felt something singing in my   chest

        empty &
     discarded

he told me once we had to stop making
love until he was ready to marry me as
though he had every kind of claim over
my body & I wonder now if he knew then
that I was not the one
        a rat in a maze
   with a chance
          to escape
a body that   wanted   to   run

---

[19] Inspired by the lyric 'she would have made such a lovely bride, what a shame she's fucked in the head' written by Taylor Swift for her song 'Champagne Problems' featuring on her album Evermore.

22

III | infidelity[20]

I danced the steps
of infidelity all along
his muscled body,

only ever in my mind—
absolved from us, I tried
to bring my daydreams
into truth.

When he
brought a smile
to my lips, I was glad
it was him,
     and not you—

I might have let
it happen, if I had
not paused to think
things through.

---

[20] *Inspired by the lyric 'do you really wanna know where I was April 29th?' written by Taylor Swift for her song 'High Infidelity' for her album Midnights: 3am Version.*

III / saint tropez[21]

Girls are not supposed to like it:
when your feelings detach and you
feel them dig their claws in.

I reigned in his efforts: petals
that would remain pressed between
the pages of my books.

Stems are left to dwindle in the futility
of knowing he was finally trying, and I,
alone in knowing that it was far too late.

I was not supposed to take centre
stage on the dating scene, gathering
my gallery of faces with relish:

we feast tonight ladies.

Nothing in this should have
settled my unease but there is
magic to be felt in being free,

on the wide, open sea.
Surrounded by bodies, yet I was
at one—anchored down
to none.

---

[21] *Inspired by the lyric 'I'd be just like Leo in Saint Tropez' written by Taylor Swift for her song 'The Man' featuring on her album Lover.*

I / too wise to trust[22]

Ghosts linger.

They are like the shape
of a bright light that clings
above your pupil, distorting
the view.

I fight the urge to shake off
my naivety when it is the only
thing that delivered him to me.

Yet here I am at twenty-three
aged to the state he found himself
in; and I know, nothing in this
world could make me

consider a love as premature
as fifteen.

In many ways now,
the power is mine. I am
older, and trust is a sustenance
rather than a sip of fine wine.

---

[22] *Inspired by the lyric 'will you forgive my soul, when you're too wise to trust me and too old to care' written by Taylor Swift for her song 'Coney Island' featuring on her album Evermore.*

25

V / demons[23]

I feel like I am covered in ivy.
It is draped across my chest and woven
around each limb, so it conceals
the entrance to a space you want to be in.

My last sweetheart said I was hard to love.
I have since been warned of the negativity
that emerges from me like tree sap—
toxic and waxy to touch. The vines are trying

to strangle me and all you can think about
is their blood on your hands. I am shrouded
from men who leave, and in turn,
any who might untangle me.

They have been enticed
only to find they are not ready,
explored my skin between the vines
and changed their minds.

Perhaps the fault is mine for discarding a love
that was perfectly fine because I simply felt nothing.
Is it better to feel nothing alongside someone
than just nothing,   with no one?

But you pulled the vines from me, so gently;
so that your fingers would not get bloody.
You laid me bare before you and asked
how has no one snapped you up yet?

And now that you cannot find a moment

---

[23] *Inspired by the lyric 'you've got your demons and, darling, they all look like me'*
written by Taylor Swift for the song 'Sad, Beautiful, Tragic' featured on her album Red
(Swift's Version).

26

to call me back, I am wondering if you might tell me how to answer that.

a fragile line[24]

Two ships pass in the stagnant glow
of night, floating in the ghosts of one
another—if it was not for the shadow
cast by the glow of a nearby lighthouse
they would be none the wiser that
the other exists.

Loving you feels like this:

futile, yet like my life depends on it
because one day you might change
course and realise there are sights
worth straying for.

There is desire and it burns me up,
makes it tempting enough to float
here forever; treading water. Yet
deep below, I know you would prefer
the girl who explored the entire ocean
before sailing back to you.

That is what I will do.

---

[24] *Inspired by the lyric 'you and I walk a fragile line' written by Taylor Swift for her song 'Haunted' featured on the album Speak Now.*

IV / left haunted[25]

I discovered him amongst
the daisies: the endless chain
we assemble with our fingers
and sift through when the
lonely sinks in.

And amongst the daisies,
fingers tinged green, he also
discovered me.

We grazed the meadow hand
in hand and I hoped I might
have found my man but he
quickly explained he didn't
care to set his roots in the
ground.

So many do not, so I understood—
although I will admit I was
disappointed.

Friendship was born and to some
may seem complicated but it works
based on one simple thing:
that he doesn't love me
yet I love him.

It may sound devastating
but all is well, daisies grow everywhere.
One man's weed will be

---

[25] Inspired by the lyric 'I wonder how many girls he has loved and left haunted' written
by Taylor Swift for her song 'Ready For It' featured on the album Reputation.

a gentleman's flower.
As much as I am wilting,
I still have the power.

I am content with dangling my feet
above the meadow grass waiting
for the chain to circle back to me
so long as there is no better place
for me to be.

IV | grinning like a devil[26]

The last time he looked me in the eyes
he was peering up from between my thighs

in my mind, I could tremble at the sight
but the aftermath lingers like a poltergeist.

I was love stained, bruising like peaches—
wanting him like I wanted the feeling

and he was aching to slip right through
my fingers. He didn't want for me in the same way,

our time long spent and trickling away.
I don't mind losing a lover, but I miss my friend.

I closed my legs and didn't hear
from him again.

---

[26] *Inspired by the lyric 'he looks up grinning like a devil' written by Taylor Swift for her song 'Cruel Summer' featured on her album Lover.*

VI | this city[27]

I am wearing my little black dress.
Lips rouged with a tint of blood orange.
You sink into a black sofa as I sip my gin
and your arm snakes its length around me.

I breathe you in. It is as though the echo
of the building we are in is whispering—
and all I hear is you.

Outside, the streetlights make your skin glow,
afire in dull, orange light and I cannot avert my eyes.
You catch me like this and there is nothing
I could do to hide even if I wanted to.

This stunning, crisp evening in early March
has me hoping that springtime is you.
I am fixated on this glow; every time
you pick me up, take me home.

There are all of these people who know your face,
but do they know how perfectly my fingertips frame it?

The outside air bites at your hands,
and I take them in my palms to soften it.
I'd wrap each one of my bones up inside your secrets—
I could build empires out of words
and you could hold them in your pockets.

Because the city is yours and I will wait
up every night for you to call and say *you are home.*

---

[27] Inspired by the lyric *'I get mystified by how this city screams your name'* written by
Taylor Swift for her song *'Cornelia Street'* featuring on her album *Lover.*

VI / *loose lips sink ships*[28]

I woke, a few moments past midnight—
that's when you came home,
folded your bones around my bones.

We talked of the difference in ways
we like to be loved.

I tiptoed around the cracks that
were once fractures in my hope.
I forced the brittle, aching structure
to consider you anyway.

There was something in the way my hand
fit around the side of your face—

something enticing in the smell of your skin,
your clothes.
The jumper I waited a week or two to wash.

Is there anything more breakable than this feeling?
Clutched in both of my hands and
I shattered it with a single blush.

Love only ever seems to grip me like this
when they press a finger to my lips
and shush me into a secret.

---

[28] *Inspired by the lyric 'loose lips sink ships all the damn time' written by Taylor Swift for her song 'I Know Places' featuring on her album 1989.*

VI / tolerated[29]

Finely sliced bell peppers,
mushrooms divided into fours,
one of those miniature bottles of wine
enough for one glass, or one sauce.

I blended our flavours carefully
and waited all day by the door—
the gleam in your eye was never for me
now I wonder what all of it was for.

Spaghetti I portioned incorrectly;
the bread was not to your taste—
you laughed about being a single man,
all our leftovers settled to waste.

So careless, the words that you whispered,
the strangest choice in time.
I was never to be yours and you,
certainly, were never mine.

---

[29] Inspired by the lyric 'my love should be celebrated but you tolerate it' written by Taylor
Swift for her song 'Tolerate It' featuring on her album Evermore.

hunting witches[30]

My face.
Hair pinned back;
skin aglow with a springtime tan—
sprawled across the chaos of her girl's group chat.

what level of quiet desperation makes a girl pose like THAT

a beg

a slag—

has he explained himself yet

says she's crazy.
won't leave him alone

She did seem the type when I met her at work.

i don't know what it is that has them all so obsessed…

they know how easily she'll open her legs

!!!

and ain't that the TRUTH

you should have heard what he said

Babe, don't leave us in suspense.

she has hearts and everything saved next to his name

---

[30] *Inspired by the lyric 'women like hunting witches too' written by Taylor Swift for her song 'Mad Woman' featuring on her album Folklore.*

35

could you get more insane?!

oh it's borderline obsessive—

but he told me: he doesn't fall in love

well it seems clear to me, she was just

a good
fuck.

untold story[31]

I have dozens of images collated
in my phone that emblazon your frame
into a ghost, imprinted on my closed eyelids.

You'll stay for a lifetime. This reverberating
love affair that failed time and time again to
materialise into something I could define.

You have all the patience in the world,
distilling me into something delicate,
the flavours just as you like them. Yet I

am impatient. My skin the pages of a
leather bound notebook waiting to be filled.
I wanted you to, but you never did.

---

[31] *Inspired by the lyric 'if you and I are a story that never gets told' written by Taylor Swift for her song 'Stay Beautiful' featured on her debut album Taylor Swift.*

VI | if a man talks shit, respond with a sonnet[32]

The ghost has come to me to say it's time
    to wake the bones that sleep beneath your sheets.
For one last time, I'll love you like you're mine.
    Temptation tastes like truth— it makes me weak.

For days, I try to coax myself away,
    the wisest of us know when time to go.
I linger on each careless word you say,
    you fool enough to think I wouldn't know.

The sunlight kissed my lips and made them swell:
    a poison apple, aching for a bite,
lodged deep inside your throat to choke farewell,
    and some might say I did it out of spite.

Yet you can never claim it was for love,
    your shallow kiss could never be enough.

---

[32] *Inspired by the lyric 'if a man talks shit then I owe him nothing' written by Taylor Swift for her song 'I Did Something Bad' featured on her album Reputation.*

VI / crazy[33]

He sits across from me, elbows bracing the table
and he remarks quite casually that I do not need to worry

about her

                                  she's crazy.

I feel myself clench my fists and almost say, but safely
think: or did you just put her through it?

Is she crazy—
or did you just need to make her a coffee?

Is she crazy—
or was she true to her thoughts?

Is she crazy—
or is she just not *one of the boys.*

Is she crazy—
or did she want to see you more
than once per week?

Is she crazy—
or did she colour her hair pink?

Is she crazy—
or did she reveal something complex?

Is she crazy—
or did she think *dating* should involve real-life dates?

---

[33] *Inspired by the lyric 'I'm crazier for you than I was at sixteen' written by Taylor
Swift for her song 'Miss Americana and the Heartbreak Prince' featured on her album
Lover.*

Is she crazy—
or was her neck a little sore from spending the night on your
single millimetre thick pillow that you bought from Home
Bargains?

Is she crazy—
or did you both want different things?

Is she crazy—
or is craziness synonymous with the kind of frustration
that bleeds through when you spend your life juggling
the aftermath of someone else's trauma only for them to
respond to yours with—

you're too much.

Is she crazy—
or did she want to be loved?

Is she crazy—
or did you tangle your fingertips into the roots of her hair
only to dangle her in your forceful grip
from such a height, her limbs became frantic
and twisted; you no longer found her attractive—
you started longing for an alternative so, instead,
you discarded her to the wind as though she was nothing
and wondered why she had the nerve to be upset?

It's hilarious to me,
you think you can double cross emotions with *crazy*,

yet you sifted through the bunch
and picked the girl who writes poetry.

VI / mastermind[34]

I set his love alight after reading; so doused
in liquor, each kiss. I pressed myself to the flame
to be reborn, like a phoenix.

His reasons were plentiful and cruel,
he blamed my loneliness which I saw as
self-sufficiency. He referenced my naivety,

he brought me to the boil by pointing
out the blush in my cheeks. So, I set his
love alight after reading.

I dropped everything—
                                        he never saw me again.

I would count my new friends like daisies
but I've run out of fingers on my hands.

---

[34] Inspired by the lyric 'what if I told you, I'm the mastermind?' written by Taylor Swift
for her song 'Mastermind' featured on her album Midnights.

unwelcome at the wake[35]

you treat all of us as though we are characters
in your poetry: sliced straight down the middle
to spread our guts across the paper and define
us how you wish

is my corpse cold enough for you to scavenge?

you are speaking as though my blood is too
dull a shade for ink—my bones too brittle to
form a quill. Instead, you exchange the love
I gave without condition for an alternate reality

I dread to think the words you have crafted
from me: do you speak of my imperfections?
the distortion of my insides from years of silently
absorbing your behaviour, the neglecting
of my feelings

it is devastating: the image in my mind of
my remains, dishevelled and splayed for your
taking, yours to cultivate into something
disturbing

your fingers cannot seem to resist churning
me, I wish you would consider leaving gracefully,
withdraw from the mess and leave me be
amongst the poetry

such that flowers might grow where the
dead are left alone

---

[35] *Inspired by the lyric 'If I am dead to you why are you at the wake?' written by Taylor Swift for her song 'My Tears Ricochet' featured on her album Folklore.*

if I had a daughter, I'd call her betty[36]

If I had a daughter, I'd call her Betty
because daughters begin like lily buds
waking in bloom to face sunlight head on.
There is strength in being as delicate as a flower,
only to be pressed between the pages of a book:
a token of love distilled in a tale of complexity.

She will be bold from the outside in
but soften—I hope she will be as soft
as the sunset yet burn like a fire.
If the best thing a girl can be in this world
is a fool, then let her be foolishly brave.

May her heart remain breakable, delicate
with each fracture that comprises a faith
daydreams.
May she protect her faith at all costs,
shying away from the bitterness
that brings about loss.

There are few things in this world worth wanting,
but she would know that to want is enough.
I want her to be more than her assets,
yet know how well she might use them.
Despite all of the things she will inevitably
lose, I will always be her friend.

If I had a daughter, I would want her
to believe in love, because it is all that I can
give her in a world where
nothing else is enough.

---

[36] *Inspired by the character 'Betty' and lyric 'Betty, I won't make assumptions' created and written by Taylor Swift for her song 'Betty' and referenced in the love triangle explored in her songs 'Cardigan,' 'August,' and 'Betty' featured on the album Folklore.*

VIII / a one night or a wife[37]

I am not sure I find solace
in either concept. The sky tonight
is purple, as though someone spilled
ink up there and I wish I could roll
around in it, tinge my skin.
Everything—
purple.

It is the only way I could know
for sure if any of it was true,
if I ever felt purple;
if I ever had you.

To me, Lavender Haze
was an incoming, and it was
okay that I wanted a pretty ring
but not a wedding.

Now it is nothing
but a purple sky and a window.
Nothing but a past life.

---

[37] *Inspired by the lyric 'the only kind of girl they see is a one night or a wife' written by Taylor Swift for her song 'Lavender Haze' featured on her album Midnights.*

a laugh I could recognise anywhere[38]

When I was eight
fearless meant singing
and daydreaming,
being slightly too loud
at the sound of music
because when it was quiet,
I would not speak at all.

At eleven,
I knew all about
fairy tales and magic
and I clung to them
in ways you might consider
vintage— a pink ipod
and a blackberry in my pocket,
with the background a photo
of her with wild, blonde curls.

At thirteen,
her lyrics began to feel
like poetry. I would sit alone
on the school bus, longing
to be twenty-two
and have the world
at my fingertips, a love
that might just be
something.
I began to long for
the familiarity
of autumn skies,

---

[38] *Inspired by the lyric 'please don't ever become a stranger whose laugh I could recognise anywhere' written by Taylor Swift for her song 'New Year's Day' featured on her album Reputation.*

the crunch of leaves
expelled from the trees.
I knew the ache
of a disappointed heart
all too well—
the way it lingers
like a daydream.

Fifteen was tricky,
plunged into a world
black and white and yearning
for colour; I was asking
for trouble. She had me
hooked on something
star-crossed
and in the end,
I was a fox in a cage.

But at least
I'd get to see her
on stage.

I was nineteen
when the two of us
emerged from the pain
like serpents poised to strike;
teeth aching for a bite.
She was more bitter
than I, but I held on
for much longer.
I bleached my hair
and coiled myself in ivy.

Then I was twenty,
I liked the darkness
of the songs, such that

when the season's changed
I was left behind.
I liked the sanctity
of melodrama seeping
from that cruel summer.
I resisted anything
as vibrant as a lover,
so I stayed with a man
who made me feel numb,
until she said
it was time to run.

I was twenty-one
and she gave me back
my daydreams,
plunged me into stories
of women who took back
their agency, treading
bare foot through trees,

I stayed in the forest
until twenty-two found me.
That winter was cold,
echoing cries from the ghosts
of lovers past and I numbed the chill
each night with a warmer kind of spirit.
In my mind,
I became the kind of woman
who might poison a lover,
just for something to do.
What else are our daydreams for?
She whispered into my ear
the hope of a better
evermore.

Now I am twenty-four

and I stay up until Midnight
with my sanctity
and my poetry—
                    and the wine.

I live in fear of the day
she does this for the very last time,
but I'll always remember
when Taylor was mine.

midnight[39]

there exists a thirteenth hour
dancing along the edge of reality
silent to most
yet all encompassing to us

it keeps us alert to the decadence
of a fading moonlight

she shimmers beneath diamond
chains and winks over her shoulder
I am older than I was when she last
took her place, and made time her own

she is distilled in a moment of
pop culture
twinkling like the glow
of a mirror ball—

that thirteenth echo reverberating
as she shares her musings
once again

what could be more powerful
than to brace your limbs upon a stage
where a man silenced you and in response
rebuild the world around you
and make yourself
the magic

we wait for her
beneath the moonlight

---

[39] *Inspired by the album Midnights from Taylor Swift.*

49

dazzled in the navy shade of midnight
I'll drink her in beside the firelight
and dance for her amongst the fireflies
I'll sing her words, again, to the stars
because we never let them take

what was ours

I'm all about you[40]

I open the window to let in the cold,
a late November chill to bite away
the ghost of an embrace.

What is there to say
aside from the refrain
I have rehearsed over and over again
for a few years and a day—

if we balance the worthy, there are simply too few
when no one could love me the way that I do.

I gather all of the moments the clock hands
allow and give every single one to myself.

I light candles on an evening, pour myself
a small glass of wine. Perform all of the rituals
that have alone become mine.

I go wherever I desire and give myself the world,
I soothe myself with lunches and matinees and pearls.

If we balance the worthy, there are simply too few
when no one can love me the way that I do.

I gave too much this time, my hope like that flower
marking where I was in the book I forgot to finish—

this is power.

---

[40] *Inspired by the lyric 'now I'm all about you' written by Taylor Swift for her song 'Long Story Short' featured on the album Evermore*

One day I will try for the very last time
and no matter what happens, all will be fine,
the weight of temptation will sit light on my mind

because if we balance the worthy, there are simply too few
when no one could love me the way that I do.

so scarlet it was...[41]

one of those memories
that burns all the way down.

I am stronger now,
my poems sprawl across
her lyrics like a
palimpsest.

I write in quill and ink,
I ache for nothing.
I write poetry that sings.

---

[41] *Inspired by the lyric 'so scarlet it was...' written by Taylor Swift for her song 'Maroon' featured on her album* Midnights.

the boys and the ballet[42]

I'd like to take Rebekah for a drink
and tell her that I think she did the right thing.

I'd like to retreat safely
into a dead man's money
and know I gave as good as I got

instead of feeling like they always
get the last laugh.

I wish I liked the taste of red wine
so, I could dress in a scarlet, satin robe
and caress the glass as though
I had just buried a man in my back garden.
I'd run my fingers over the keys of his piano.
I would not know how to play the piano
but I would know how to kill my lovers
in a way that miraculously
raises no suspicion.

I would know
to only use weapons
they had to swallow,
make it look like an ailment,
a heart attack— fain sorrow.

No one would ever suspect
a thing.

---

[42] *Inspired by the lyric 'blew through the money on the boys and the ballet' written by Taylor Swift for her song 'The Last Great American Dynasty' featured on her album Folklore. Lyric 'I had a marvellous time ruining everything' is also sampled from the song.*

I could elongate my limbs
across his vintage, hand woven couch
and entertain gentlemen,
give them the keys
to his house—
then change the locks
before they get too
comfortable,

make them disappear
if they feel
too lovable.

And a smile will
perk up from the corner
of my mouth,
and no one will dare
to say a thing—

because I learned from Rebekah Harkness
                              and I win.

*I had a marvellous time
ruining
everything.*

lonesome I came[43]

I was pulling poems together with
my fingertips when the cavalry came
and sent us home. My fair weather friends
scattered across the rail lines, linked
by aching metal and tiny black screens.

In my dreams, we never left. We're still
cross legged in our city, sipping coffee
and sharing words in our own little ways.
The only real thing is the poetry—I have
a shelf of successes where I used to
sit photographs.

The world moved again eventually, the
creaking tracks pulling us forward,
moving us back—I'm still sat
where the solitude left me.
Encapsulated by the ghost of what
once was but can never again be.

We are scattered like dandelion feathers.
We could settle anywhere and become
something new. I have strayed from
the path, barefoot in the wild grass.
I am muddying my feet.

It's me. Just myself; alone as a flower,
and now I have realised—*lonely is power.*

---

[43] *Inspired by the lyric 'lost I was born, lonesome I came, lonesome I always stay' written by Taylor Swift for the song 'Carolina' featured in the 2022 film Where the Crawdads Sing.*

56

Lyrics

The first way in which Taylor Swift inspired me to write
was with lyrics.

Between the ages of 13 and 18 I performed my favourite
covers and original songs around Moreton-In-Marsh,
Stratford Upon Avon and the surrounding areas.

Writing in this way was undoubtedly my first experience of
writing poetry; it feels fitting to print the lyrics I am most
proud of as an epilogue to this book.

It is unlikely that I will sing them again.

Fingerprints

I'm retracing steps to get back where we were
back when *I'll put you first* was the biggest lie I'd ever heard.
And I gave you all I could
and I loved more than any girl should
but when it comes to scarlet letters, you see,
the blame is on me.

But did you ever stop and think
maybe we were worth more than this?
It's hard to let go of sinking ships
when I never thought we'd have a last kiss.

There's so many foreign hands involved trying to find a root
cause,
when they dusted me off for fingerprints, they only found
yours.
So you see, my love, I don't what else I can do.
Because when it comes to the fall of us,
the blame is on you.

But did you ever stop and think
maybe we were worth more than this?
It's hard to let go of sinking ships
when I never thought we'd have a last kiss
and I'd follow you to the ends of the earth
but you walk faster than I could run.
I don't want to brush your fingerprints from my skin,
but it's time to let the parting sink in.

You see my darling,
it was apparent to me from the start,
people make movies
about this kind of love.

But did you ever stop and think,
maybe she deserves better than this?
I don't want to abandon our sinking ship
when I never thought we'd have a last kiss
and I'd follow you to the ends of the earth
but you walk faster than I could run.
And I don't want to brush your fingerprints from my skin,
but it's time to let the parting sink in.

Walls & Oceans

You know it's in the back of my mind;
I know you can see it in my eyes.
I can always anticipate changing minds
but we're hand in hand,
chest to chest,
four brown eyes.

I feel like pebble in the ocean
just trying to get back to shore
and you're holding back the tempest
because we both know I won't survive the storm.
And the rain is coming down,
and I'm counting on you now.

Because I built walls
and I've burned bridges
and it feels like I'm clutching at straws
just trying to be something
you adore.
And nothing more.

It's not your fault,
I've been bruised.
And it's not my fault
there's something about you.

But a scar isn't going to fade
in a few months and as many days
doesn't mean I'm not trying to stay.

Because I've built walls
and I've burned bridges
and it feels like I'm clutching at straws
just trying to be something

you adore.
And pick our bleeding hearts
up off the floor.

Because the rains really pouring now.
Don't let me down.

Endorsements

Luke Kennard, author of Notes on the Sonnets

A joyfully inventive work of intertextuality, ricocheting off Swift's music and lyrics to create a sequence of biography, memoir and defiance which wrestles with story, identity, originals and versions."

Betty Doyle, author of Girl Parts

She and I. Her and Me

and so the deft and delicate poems in Swift Happenings explore a relationship recognized by many, between the power of Taylor Swift's music and the hearts of millions. Throughout this collection, Hanks employs numerous recognizable Swift tropes to her own affect— these poems brim with bedrooms, rain, daydreams and storybooks, love oaths and double-edged swords, ghosts and red lips and streetlights and midnights, magic and secrets and aching and independence. This collection shines through its sincere expression of love towards Swift and her creations with a special focus on the much-aligned yet vital and powerful experience of young womanhood, treating them with delicacy and respect, allowing their feminine power to command the space and dazzle. These are important poems, not just for Swift fans, but as a testimony to the happiness, freedom, loneliness, and confusion that define the lives of the people that will take over the world— teenage girls.

Thanks

My opportunity to finally comprise my love of Taylor Swift into something tangible came whilst I was enrolled on the Creative Writing MA with the University of Birmingham. Therefore, I firstly thank my cohort. You were the most unique and creatively empowered group of people I have ever met or had the pleasure to work with. Not a moment went by where I didn't know how lucky I was to be writing with you all and our shared support of each other has been my favourite takeaway from the entire experience.

Furthermore, I thank Elle Desatge, Laura Stanley, Bunmi Famuyiwa, and Ben Welsh for their dedicated and careful feedback during our group dissertation supervision sessions. You were all writing such stunning and poignant poetry, and I was bringing my youth-filled, daydream-esque, Swiftie-inspired poems and you never lost patience with me. Thank you.

To Dr Isabel Galleymore, a poet I so admire and respect, for her consistent and supportive supervision of this project. Also, to Dr Luke Kennard for always offering encouragement and enthusiasm for my poetry whilst enrolled on the course and beyond. It was a pleasure and joy to work with you both.

As always, thanks to Dr Jack McGowan. I am not sure if Jack realised when appointed as my personal academic tutor in the second year of my undergraduate degree that his role would last a lifetime, but I do not intend on letting him go any time soon. I am eternally grateful for your continued support and friendship.

Lastly, to Taylor. I wish I could sum it up into something poignant and powerful, but you have been the single constant thing I have had since I was a child. I wouldn't know where to begin with thanking you. I hope this book is a start.

Previous Publications

May We All Be Artefacts, (*V. Press Poetry*, 2021)
I Call Upon the Witches*, (Sunday Mornings at the River*, 2022)

also featured in:

Poetry in the Time of Coronavirus, 'The Great Slumber,'
(*Independently published by G.A. Cuddy,* 2020)
Hair-Raising: an anthology, 'Brunette with just a Touch of
Red' (*Nine Pens Press*, 2021)
Elements Natural and the Supernatural: an anthology, 'A
Midsummer Night's Dream,' 'Long Nights,' and 'The Forest'
(*Fawn Press*, 2021)
Depression Is What Really Killed the Dinosaurs, 'Blood
Letting,' 'Joan,' and 'The Hanging Tree' (*Sunday Mornings at the
River*, 2022)
The Confessions Anthology, 'Proud' (*WordSpace*, 2022)

Printed in Great Britain
by Amazon

18162277R00047